J.S. BACH

10 Pieces Transcribed for Piano
by
Wilhelm Kempff

ISBN 978-0-7935-5726-4

Associated Music Publishers, Inc.

DISTRIBUTED BY
HAL•LEONARD®
CORPORATION
7777 W. BLUEMOUND RD. P.O. BOX 13819 MILWAUKEE, WI 53213

Wilhelm Kempff was born in Jüterbog, Germany, in 1895. His parents were distinguished musicians. From the age of nine he studied piano and composition at the Berlin Hochschule für Musik, and the Viktoriagymnasium in Potsdam. He also studied philosophy and music history. In 1916, he began to concertize and became renowned throughout Europe, South America and Japan as one of the leading pianists of our time. He made his debut in English speaking countries rather late in his career; in London in 1951 and in New York in 1964. Kempff has achieved international fame with his interpretations of Classical and Romantic music, particlularly Beethoven's sonatas, and has recorded much of his repertory.

CONTENTS

To Albert Schweitzer

Siciliano
from the Flute Sonata No. 2

J. S. Bach (BWV 1031)

To Albert Schweitzer

Largo
from the Piano Concerto in F Minor

J. S. Bach (BWV 1056)

Organ Chorale: Command Your Way
"I Am Anxiously Longing"

J. S. Bach (BWV 727)

Very supported, *with simple expression*
Lento e legatissimo

moving forward
legato marcato

This Organ Chorale, originating from the Krebs legacy, is to be played with a simple legato. The pedal should be touched only sparingly and should not be misused to create a pseudo-legato.

AMP-7819-3

The transcriber prefers this canonic version.

To Edwin Fischer

Prelude to the Ratswahl Cantata
"We thank you, God, we thank you"

J. S. Bach (BWV 29)

Copyright © 1931, 1959 Bote & Bock, Berlin   All Rights Reserved.

Chorale from the Cantata:
Heart and Mouth and Deed and Life
"Jesus, Joy of Man's Desiring"

J. S. Bach (BWV 147)

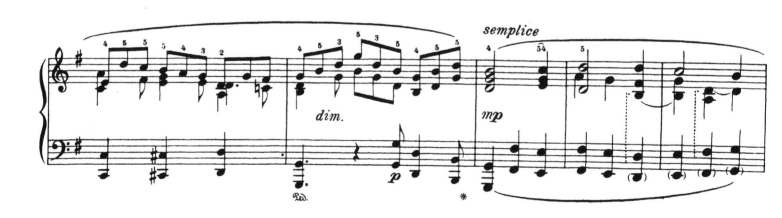

*The transcriber omits the playing of the chorale at this place.

AMP-7819-3

Chorale Prelude:
I Call to You, Lord Jesus Christ

J. S. Bach (BWV 639)

Chorale Prelude:
The Saviour of the Heathen now Comes

J. S. Bach (BWV 659a)

The Saviour of the heathen now comes,
He who is known as the Child of the Virgin!
All the world wonders that
God should ordain such a birth.
From the Latin of his holiness Ambrosius (Martin) Luther, 1524

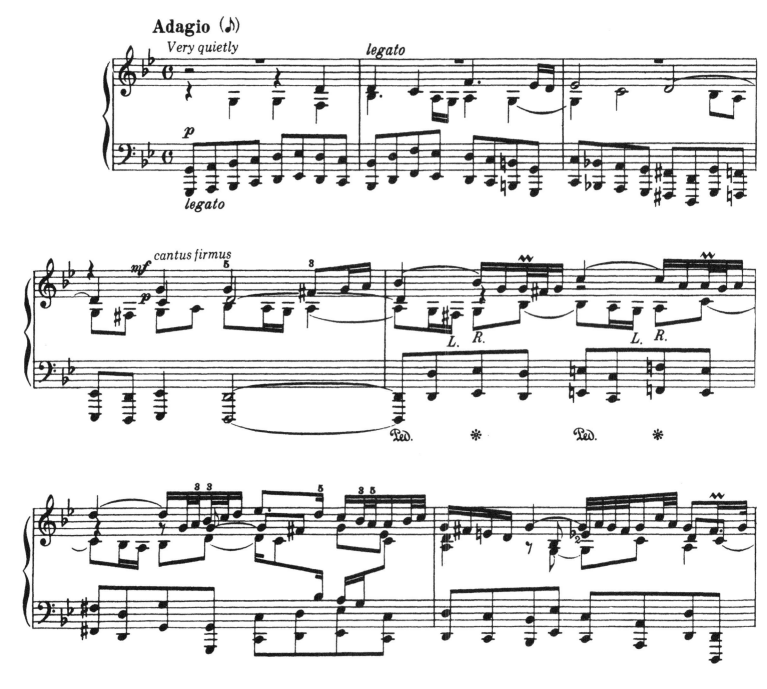

Chorale Prelude:
In Sweet Rejoicing

J. S. Bach (BWV 751)

Joyfully moving (*Allegro giocoso*)

AMP-7819-3

*The treble should have the silvery light sound of an organ 4 foot stop. The pedal must be used with great care.

AMP-7819-3

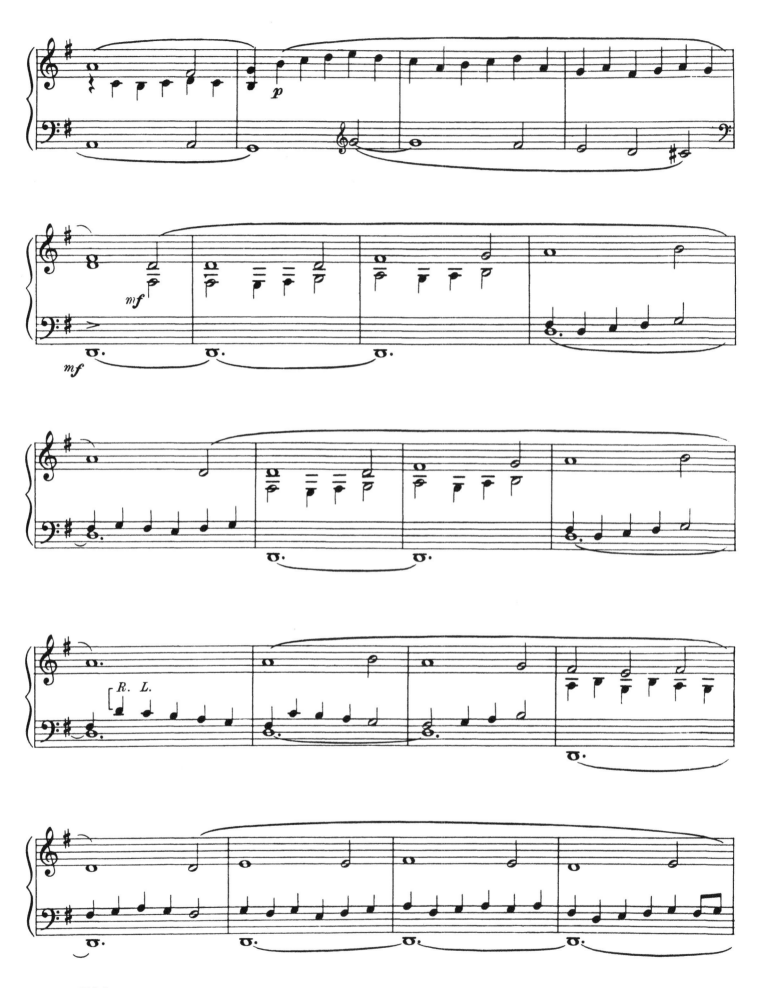

Chorale Prelude:
Awake, the Voice is Sounding

J. S. Bach (BWV 645)

Zion hears the watchman singing,
Her beating heart with joy is springing,
She wakens and with speed arises.
Her friend appears in heaven's glory,
Strong in Grace, in truth his story,
His light is bright, his star surprises.
Now come, you worthy crown,
Lord Jesus, God's own Son!
Hosannah!
We all follow
To the hall of joy beyond compare,
The Lord's own Supper there to share!

Chorale Prelude:
It is Surely the Time
Now Rejoice, My Beloved Christ

J. S. Bach (BWV 307 & 734)

CHORALE

Broad, strong *Largamente, forte*

*The transcriber plays the repeat *piano* on the second Manual.

AMP-7819-3

CHORALE PRELUDE

Joyfully moving (*allegramente mosso*) (♩ = ♪)